Business Is Business

The Unspoken Rules of Success

Ghazwan Alemara

Copyright © 2024 Ghazwan Alemara. All rights reserved.

No part of this publication may be reproduced, distributed, or transmitted in any form or by any means, including photocopying, recording, or other electronic or mechanical methods, without the prior written permission of the publisher, except in the case of brief quotations embodied in critical reviews and certain other noncommercial uses permitted by copyright law.

For permissions requests or inquiries, please contact the publisher at hello@ghazwanalemara.com

Published by ghazwanalemara.com

Contents

Contents 3
Introduction 1
The Hidden Language of Business 3
    Non-Verbal Communication in Negotiations 3
    Reading Between the Lines in Contracts 7
    The Power of Listening 10
Relationships Over Transactions 15
    Building Trust Before the Deal 15
    The Long Game in Networking 18
    The Invisible Network 22
Emotional Resilience as a Business Skill 27
    Handling Rejection and Setbacks 27
    The Calm Leader in a Storm 31
    Cultivating a Resilient Mindset 34
Timing is Everything 39
    Recognizing Market Opportunities 39
    Knowing When to Walk Away 43
    The Right Time to Expand 46
The Ethics of Profit 52
    Balancing Integrity and Profit 52
    Corporate Social Responsibility (CSR) as a Growth Tool 55
    Avoiding the Trap of Cutting Corners 59
The Unseen Cost of Success 63

- Burnout Among Business Leaders 63
- Sacrifices That Shouldn't Be Made.................................. 67
- Sustainable Success 70

The Power of Small Wins 75
- Celebrating Milestones 75
- Building Momentum from Minor Successes 78
- The Compound Effect in Business 82

Innovating in a Saturated Market 86
- Differentiating Through Customer Experience............ 86
- The Unspoken Rule of Simplicity................................. 90
- Continuous Innovation as a Mindset 93

Mastering the Art of Quiet Influence.................................. 98
- Leading Without Titles 98
- Creating Change from Behind the Scenes................ 101
- The Subtle Art of Persuasion..................................... 105

Success Without Sacrificing Values 110
- The True Definition of Success 110
- Building a Legacy, Not Just a Business.................... 113
- The Legacy of Leadership... 116

Conclusion... 120

Introduction

There's a world in business that isn't captured in textbooks, podcasts, or seminars. It's the world behind boardroom doors, woven into silent gestures and subtle decisions, where unspoken rules often determine who rises and who falls. These rules, overlooked by many but followed religiously by the successful, form the essence of what makes a business thrive. Yet, few ever talk about them.

In this book, we pull back the curtain on these hidden principles. We explore the strategies, relationships, and insights that the most successful business leaders employ but rarely discuss. Whether it's understanding the quiet power of influence, the timing of key decisions, or the delicate balance between ethics and profitability, this book provides a deep dive into what it really takes to win in business.

At its core, this book aims to do more than just inform. It seeks to shift your perspective on business, showing you how to navigate with confidence through complexities, where it's not just about what you know, but how well you understand the game. Each chapter offers practical guidance, actionable insights, and real-world examples to help you put these rules into practice, whether you're an aspiring entrepreneur, a seasoned executive, or somewhere in between.

The importance of these unspoken rules has never been greater. In a rapidly changing market, where competition is fierce and expectations are high, it's the small, often unnoticed moves that make the biggest difference. The ability to see beyond the obvious and understand what truly drives success gives you a competitive edge.

Throughout this book, you will journey through ten chapters, each focusing on a different aspect of these hidden rules. From mastering non-verbal communication to leveraging relationships over transactions, and from understanding the unseen costs of success to the subtle art of persuasion, you'll discover strategies that few talk about, but many successful leaders follow. Along the way, you'll learn how to align these strategies with your values, ensuring that you not only achieve success but do so without losing yourself in the process.

By the time you finish this book, you won't just be better informed, you'll be equipped to navigate the intricate and often murky waters of business with newfound clarity. You'll know the moves to make, the pitfalls to avoid, and the unspoken rules that will guide you toward long-term success.

Chapter 1

The Hidden Language of Business

Non-Verbal Communication in Negotiations

When you walk into a negotiation, the conversation starts long before the first word is spoken. Your handshake, posture, and even the way you make eye contact send signals that set the tone for the discussion. Non-verbal communication often has more impact than the words exchanged in a negotiation. Understanding and mastering these subtle cues can give you an edge in any business situation.

The Power of Presence

First impressions are crucial. From the moment you enter the room, your presence can convey confidence or insecurity, openness or defensiveness. A firm handshake, steady eye contact, and a calm demeanor can immediately establish you as someone to be taken seriously. People naturally respond to what they perceive, so showing confidence without arrogance builds trust.

Your body language should also be open and engaged. Standing or sitting up straight, avoiding crossed arms, and maintaining a relaxed posture shows that you are approachable and willing to collaborate. On the other hand, slouching or fidgeting can convey disinterest or discomfort, which can lead to a loss of control in the negotiation.

Reading the Room

It's not just about what you communicate—it's about what others are communicating as well. The ability to read the non-verbal cues of your counterpart can help you gauge their true feelings. Are they leaning forward, indicating engagement, or are they leaning back, signaling hesitation? Notice their eye contact—consistent and direct eye contact usually indicates confidence, while avoiding eye contact can suggest uncertainty or dishonesty.

Watch for micro-expressions, those fleeting facial reactions that reveal a person's true emotions before they can mask them. A brief flicker of frustration or surprise can give you insight into their thought process. If someone raises an eyebrow or tightens their lips after a proposal, it could signal that they're not as comfortable with the offer as they let on.

Mirroring for Connection

Mirroring is a powerful tactic for building rapport. When you subtly mimic the body language of the person you're negotiating with, it creates a sense of connection. People tend to feel more comfortable with those who resemble them, even in small ways. If your counterpart leans forward, you can also lean forward slightly. If they nod their head while listening, you can reflect that same movement. This creates a subconscious sense of understanding, which can lead to more favorable outcomes.

However, it's important to do this naturally. Forced mirroring can come off as insincere or manipulative, which will work against you. The goal is to make the other person feel understood and at ease, not to mimic them robotically.

Controlling the Flow of the Conversation

Body language also plays a role in controlling the flow of the negotiation. Small gestures, like leaning in slightly when you make a key point, can signal that what you're about to say is important. Pausing before responding shows that you are thoughtful, while maintaining eye contact during those moments reinforces your confidence in what you are saying.

On the other hand, leaning back or breaking eye contact during a tense moment can create distance, giving you time to think or giving the other person room to reconsider their position. Being aware of how you use space and movement can help you subtly guide the conversation.

The Silent Signals of Power

Power dynamics in negotiations often manifest through non-verbal cues. For example, taking up more physical space by spreading out materials or leaning comfortably back in a chair can convey dominance. A more dominant negotiator might also initiate the handshake or control the pace of the conversation with pauses or measured speech.

Even silence is a powerful tool. Holding a thoughtful pause after the other person speaks forces them to fill the space, often revealing more than they intended. This can be particularly useful when the other party is uncertain about their position, as silence can create subtle pressure.

Mastering non-verbal communication in negotiations is about more than just appearing confident. It's about reading the subtle signals in the room, understanding how your body language affects others, and using those cues to build trust, assert power, and influence the outcome. Every movement and gesture adds depth to the conversation, often revealing more than words ever could. In the world of business, where the stakes are high and competition fierce, mastering these silent signals can be the difference between success and failure.

Reading Between the Lines in Contracts

Contracts are the backbone of any business transaction, outlining the terms, expectations, and obligations of all parties involved. However, while the obvious clauses may seem straightforward, it's the subtleties hidden within the legal language that often carry the most weight. Knowing how to "read between the lines" in contracts is an essential skill for anyone navigating the business world.

Spotting Ambiguity

One of the most important things to watch out for in any contract is ambiguous language. Words like "reasonable," "appropriate," or "best efforts" may seem harmless, but they can create significant gray areas. What is "reasonable" to one party may not be reasonable to another, and this ambiguity can lead to disputes later on. When you encounter vague language, ask for clarification or revisions. A well-drafted contract should be precise, leaving no room for misinterpretation.

Hidden Risks in "Boilerplate" Clauses

Boilerplate clauses are those standard, often overlooked sections found at the end of many contracts, like indemnity, jurisdiction, or dispute resolution. These might seem like standard language, but they can hold significant consequences. For instance, an indemnity clause may shift the financial burden to one party in unforeseen situations, while a jurisdiction clause can determine where legal disputes are resolved, potentially in an inconvenient or costly location for your business. It's critical to review these clauses carefully and understand their implications before signing.

Pay Attention to "Force Majeure"

A common, yet often underappreciated, clause is the "force majeure" provision, which allows parties to avoid liability for obligations due to unforeseen events, such as natural disasters or political unrest. While it's reasonable to include this clause, it's essential to understand the scope. Make sure the list of covered events isn't overly broad, as it could provide the other party with too many opportunities to escape their obligations.

Beware of "Evergreen" Clauses

Another potential pitfall is the "evergreen" clause, which automatically renews the contract unless a party takes specific action to terminate it. While convenient, this can lock you into agreements longer than anticipated if you don't remember to provide timely notice. These clauses are easy to miss, so always check for automatic renewal terms and plan ahead to avoid unwanted extensions.

Penalties and Early Termination Fees

Pay close attention to termination clauses, particularly those involving penalties or early termination fees. Some contracts include steep financial penalties for ending the agreement early, which can be a costly oversight. Always review these clauses with an eye toward your long-term flexibility. A rigid contract can hurt your business if circumstances change, and you're stuck in an unfavorable agreement.

The Importance of Thorough Review

Finally, never assume that standard contracts are in your favor. Even in long-standing business relationships, it's vital to review each contract carefully before signing. Consulting a legal professional is always a good idea, especially when you're unsure about the implications of certain clauses. Contracts are meant to protect your interests, so ensure every part of the agreement works for you, not against you.

Reading between the lines of a contract isn't just about understanding what's on the page, but also about recognizing what's missing, what's unclear, and what could potentially pose a risk to your business down the road. By approaching each contract with diligence and attention to detail, you can avoid unpleasant surprises and protect your business interests effectively.

The Power of Listening

In business, it's easy to get caught up in the idea that the most successful people are those who speak the most or dominate a conversation. However, true influence often comes from mastering the art of listening. Listening isn't just about hearing words; it's about understanding what's behind those words, picking up on underlying concerns, motivations, and emotions. In fact, listening can be one of the most powerful tools in a negotiator's or leader's arsenal, setting the foundation for stronger relationships, better decision-making, and ultimately, more successful outcomes.

Listening Builds Trust

Trust is the currency of any business relationship, and the quickest way to build trust is through active listening. When you listen to someone, really listen, you signal that you value their input, opinions, and perspective. People are more likely to open up when they feel heard, which not only fosters a positive relationship but also allows for a deeper understanding of their needs and priorities. This is particularly important in negotiations, where understanding the other side's concerns and motivations can lead to mutually beneficial outcomes.

Leaders who prioritize listening over talking often inspire greater loyalty and collaboration within their teams. Employees who feel that their voices are heard are more likely to be engaged, motivated, and willing to go the extra mile. Listening shows respect and demonstrates that you're not just interested in pushing your own agenda, but in finding solutions that work for everyone.

Gathering Information Without Asking

Listening allows you to gather valuable information that might not be explicitly stated. People often reveal more than they realize when they talk, especially in the nuances of how they say something. Pauses, shifts in tone, or hesitations can give you clues about what they're truly thinking, even if they're trying to present a confident front.

For example, if a business partner hesitates when discussing a project deadline, it might indicate uncertainty or hidden concerns about meeting it. By picking up on that hesitation and asking a follow-up question, you can uncover potential problems before they escalate. In a negotiation, carefully listening to how a counterpart frames their offers or concerns can reveal their bottom line or flexibility, giving you an edge in crafting a successful deal.

Listening as a Leadership Skill

For leaders, listening is not just about gathering information—it's about empowering others. When team members know that their ideas and concerns are genuinely considered, they are more likely to contribute their best thinking. Listening creates an environment where innovation can flourish, and it also ensures that leaders are aware of what's happening on the ground level. Many business failures result from leaders being disconnected from the realities faced by their teams, simply because they weren't listening.

Listening also helps in conflict resolution. By giving both sides in a dispute the opportunity to express their viewpoints without interruption, a leader can create the space for productive dialogue. More often than not, conflicts arise from misunderstandings or feelings of being ignored. Leaders who listen actively can de-escalate tension, clarify miscommunications, and guide their teams toward resolution.

Listening as a Negotiation Tactic

Negotiation is often thought of as a battle of wits, where the person who talks the most or pushes the hardest wins. However, the best negotiators know that listening is their most effective tool. By letting the other person speak more, you not only gather essential information but also allow them to feel like they are in control. This often leads to them revealing more than they intended or giving away critical pieces of the puzzle that help you craft a stronger counteroffer.

In addition, when the other side feels heard, they are more likely to be open to compromise. Instead of entering a negotiation with the goal of winning, listening helps you find common ground. It shifts the dynamic from adversarial to collaborative, allowing both parties to work toward a solution that benefits everyone.

Listening may seem passive, but it is one of the most active and effective skills you can develop in business. It helps you build trust, gather critical information, lead more effectively, and negotiate smarter deals. The next time you're in a business meeting or negotiation, resist the urge to dominate the conversation. Instead, focus on listening, and watch how the dynamics change in your favor.

Chapter 2

Relationships Over Transactions

Building Trust Before the Deal

Trust is the foundation of every successful business relationship. Before any deal is signed, trust needs to be established. Without it, even the most promising opportunities can quickly fall apart. In the fast-paced world of business, building trust early sets the tone for everything that follows, ensuring smoother negotiations, stronger partnerships, and long-term success.

The First Impression Matters

Trust often begins with the first impression. How you present yourself, your business, and your intentions during initial interactions will shape the perception others have of you. Being authentic and transparent from the outset is key. Whether in face-to-face meetings, email exchanges, or video conferences, maintaining a professional yet approachable demeanor sets the stage for a relationship built on trust.

Be mindful of how you communicate. People are more likely to trust someone who listens as much as they speak. Take the time to understand the other party's needs, concerns, and goals. This shows that you're not just looking to benefit yourself but are genuinely interested in a mutually beneficial outcome.

Transparency and Honesty

The quickest way to erode trust is by hiding information or being vague about critical details. If there are challenges or potential issues in your offer, it's better to be upfront about them. Honesty builds credibility. When the other party knows you're not withholding anything, they're more likely to reciprocate with openness. This transparency extends to your business practices, pricing, and any potential risks associated with the deal.

While it may be tempting to downplay difficulties or inflate your capabilities, being straightforward about what you can realistically deliver fosters respect. It's far better to under-promise and over-deliver than to set expectations you can't meet.

Consistency in Actions and Communication

Trust isn't built in a single interaction. It grows over time through consistent behavior. When your actions align with your words, you demonstrate reliability. If you say you'll send a proposal by Friday, ensure it's in their inbox on time. If you commit to a follow-up meeting, make it happen as scheduled. Small actions like these build a track record of dependability.

Consistency also applies to how you communicate. Be clear, concise, and responsive. Avoid giving mixed signals or changing your position without explanation. In business, consistency is the glue that holds relationships together, showing that you're someone who can be relied upon, no matter the circumstances.

Offering Value Without Expectation

One of the most effective ways to build trust before a deal is by providing value without expecting immediate returns. This could be as simple as offering insights, advice, or even connections that might help the other party. When you contribute to their success without strings attached, it shows that you're invested in the relationship beyond just closing the deal. It also signals that you're a long-term thinker, focused on building partnerships rather than one-off transactions.

People remember those who help them when there's nothing to gain. This goodwill often leads to stronger, more enduring business relationships.

Demonstrating Integrity

Finally, trust is built on integrity. Conducting yourself with strong moral principles—whether it's honoring confidentiality, treating others with respect, or doing the right thing even when it's difficult—cements your reputation as someone worthy of trust. Business deals come and go, but integrity leaves a lasting impression that can open doors for future opportunities.

Building trust before a deal takes effort, but it's an investment that pays off in every aspect of business. When trust is established early, negotiations flow more smoothly, problems are resolved more quickly, and partnerships last longer. Trust isn't just a benefit—it's the foundation of business success.

The Long Game in Networking

In the business world, networking is often portrayed as a quick means to an end—a way to land a deal, find a job, or close a partnership. But the most successful business leaders know that real networking is a long game. It's not about immediate returns or transactional relationships. Instead, it's about cultivating deep, genuine connections that grow and flourish over time, often paying off in unexpected ways.

Building Relationships, Not Just Contacts

The key to long-term networking success is shifting your mindset from accumulating contacts to building relationships. It's easy to exchange business cards or connect on LinkedIn, but those interactions alone don't form a meaningful network. What really matters is investing in the relationship beyond that initial meeting.

Building relationships means showing genuine interest in people—understanding their goals, challenges, and values. When you take the time to understand someone on a deeper level, you're creating a foundation of trust and mutual respect. This foundation is far more valuable than any surface-level connection, as it positions you as someone who is not only a resource but a true partner in their success.

Consistency Over Time

One of the most overlooked aspects of networking is the importance of consistency. Relationships, like anything valuable, require maintenance. You can't expect to build a strong network by only reaching out when you need something. The long game means staying in touch, offering help when it's not expected, and checking in without a hidden agenda.

For example, sending a quick message to congratulate someone on a career milestone or sharing a relevant article with them can go a long way. These small, consistent actions remind people that you value the relationship, not just when it's convenient for you. Over time, this consistency builds goodwill, which often leads to opportunities down the road—sometimes when you least expect it.

Offering Value Without Expectation

One of the most powerful ways to nurture long-term relationships is by offering value without expecting anything in return. This could mean sharing knowledge, connecting someone with a helpful contact, or offering support when they face a challenge. People remember those who help them without an immediate ask, and this type of generosity often pays dividends over time.

The most valuable networks are built on reciprocity and trust. When you invest in others by giving more than you take, people are naturally inclined to return the favor. While the payoff might not be immediate, this approach fosters lasting relationships that can yield opportunities and collaborations down the road.

Playing the Long Game in Career Advancement

The long game in networking isn't just about potential business deals. It's also essential for career growth. Your network is an ecosystem of mentors, peers, and colleagues who can support and guide you throughout your career. Over time, as you advance and your network grows, these connections can lead to unexpected job offers, partnerships, or even advice that helps you navigate a tricky professional situation.

Rather than rushing to expand your network, focus on nurturing relationships with people who share your values and vision. The quality of your connections is far more important than the quantity. These relationships can open doors that you didn't even know existed when the time is right.

Staying Top of Mind

The beauty of the long game in networking is that by being consistent and offering value, you stay top of mind without being pushy. When a need arises, whether it's a recommendation, a job opening, or a potential collaboration, people are more likely to think of you if you've remained present in their professional life. Being there, even in small ways, ensures that when opportunities emerge, you're not a distant memory but a trusted contact who they feel comfortable reaching out to.

The long game requires patience, consistency, and genuine interest in others. But in the end, it leads to a network that not only supports your business and career but one that fosters mutual success for all involved.

The Invisible Network

In the world of business, much of the focus tends to be on high-profile connections—investors, CEOs, and big-name clients. However, beneath the surface exists a quieter, yet equally powerful force: the invisible network. This network is composed of individuals who work behind the scenes, those who may never receive the spotlight but play an essential role in your business's success. These are the mentors, advisors, accountants, and even assistants who ensure that everything runs smoothly. Learning how to tap into this invisible network can be a game changer for any business.

The Importance of Behind-the-Scenes Players

Business success rarely happens in isolation. There's often a group of dedicated professionals working in the background, providing essential support and guidance. For example, a trusted accountant who ensures your finances are in order may not be someone you showcase in board meetings, but their work is crucial to avoiding costly mistakes. Likewise, an administrative assistant who handles scheduling and correspondence might not make the headlines, but their organizational skills keep things running like clockwork.

These individuals often possess deep institutional knowledge, offering valuable insights that others might overlook. By recognizing and engaging with these key behind-the-scenes players, you can create a stronger foundation for your business. Their expertise and loyalty are often underappreciated but can be the backbone of long-term success.

Building Relationships with Silent Supporters

While most business leaders invest time in cultivating visible relationships with clients and partners, it's equally important to nurture relationships with your invisible network. This means taking the time to acknowledge and appreciate those who contribute to your success from behind the curtain. A simple gesture of appreciation or a quick check-in with your accountant or legal advisor can go a long way toward building trust and loyalty.

It's also important to seek their advice actively. Because these individuals often have a deep understanding of the inner workings of your business, they may provide valuable perspectives that can guide key decisions. Listening to their advice not only strengthens your relationship but also helps you make better-informed choices.

Mentorship and Advisory Roles

A significant part of your invisible network can come from mentors and advisors—people who may not be directly involved in your day-to-day operations but provide critical guidance. These individuals often bring years of experience and can offer a fresh perspective on challenges you might face. Their advice, while not always glamorous or public, can prevent major missteps and help navigate difficult decisions.

It's important to cultivate a strong relationship with these mentors, seeking their counsel regularly and respecting their expertise. Their role may not be visible to the rest of your team or clients, but their impact on your business's direction can be profound.

Leveraging the Network for Growth

The invisible network isn't just about maintaining the status quo; it can also be a powerful engine for growth. Whether it's a legal advisor offering insight on how to expand into a new market or an experienced mentor helping you pivot your business model, the behind-the-scenes players can open doors to new opportunities.

Additionally, many of these connections have their own networks, which you can leverage for introductions, partnerships, or even new clients. Don't underestimate the influence that your invisible network holds. By nurturing these relationships, you can tap into a wealth of opportunities that might otherwise remain hidden.

Understanding and embracing the power of your invisible network can transform the way you approach business. These are the unsung heroes of your operation, quietly working behind the scenes to ensure that everything runs smoothly and efficiently. Recognizing their value and maintaining strong relationships with them will not only make your business more resilient but also help you seize opportunities for growth that others might miss.

Chapter 3

Emotional Resilience as a Business Skill

Handling Rejection and Setbacks

In business, setbacks and rejections are inevitable. Whether it's a deal that falls through, an idea that gets turned down, or a project that fails, everyone faces moments when things don't go according to plan. How you handle these moments is often what sets successful people apart from the rest. Learning to bounce back from rejection with resilience and a clear mind is an essential skill in any business environment.

Shifting Perspective

The first step in handling rejection is to reframe how you see it. Instead of viewing rejection as a personal failure, see it as part of the process. No one gets every deal, job, or opportunity they pursue. Rejection is simply a signal that there's more to learn, adjust, or try. By shifting your perspective from "I failed" to "This didn't work, but I can learn from it," you take back control of the situation. This mindset change allows you to see setbacks not as roadblocks, but as stepping stones toward eventual success.

Many successful entrepreneurs and leaders faced numerous rejections before they achieved their goals. What they had in common was their ability to keep going, adapt, and not take rejection personally. It's important to remind yourself that rejection isn't a reflection of your worth—it's simply part of the journey.

Emotional Resilience

Rejection often triggers an emotional response, and that's completely normal. It can feel frustrating, disappointing, and even disheartening at times. However, building emotional resilience helps you recover faster and move forward with greater clarity. Emotional resilience doesn't mean ignoring your feelings; it means allowing yourself to experience them while maintaining perspective.

One effective way to build emotional resilience is by practicing self-compassion. When a setback occurs, instead of being overly critical of yourself, treat yourself with kindness. Acknowledge the disappointment, but also recognize that setbacks happen to everyone. This approach helps prevent the spiral of negative self-talk that can hold you back from trying again.

Learning from Setbacks

Every setback has something to teach you if you're willing to look for the lesson. After experiencing a rejection, take time to analyze what went wrong and what could be improved. Did the timing of your proposal misalign with the other party's needs? Was there a miscommunication or misunderstanding? Was your strategy lacking in some way?

By breaking down the rejection and identifying the factors that contributed to it, you gain valuable insights that can inform your next move. This kind of analysis not only helps you avoid similar mistakes in the future but also gives you the confidence to approach the next opportunity with more wisdom and preparation.

Persistence is Key

Setbacks often test your persistence. The ability to keep going after a rejection is what separates those who eventually succeed from those who give up. Persistence doesn't mean stubbornly pursuing the same approach; it means staying committed to your broader goals, even when the path to achieving them requires changes in direction.

Consider how many businesses that are successful today were built on multiple failed attempts. Whether it's launching new products, seeking investors, or building client relationships, every opportunity comes with a risk of rejection. Those who persist, adapt, and learn from each rejection are the ones who ultimately break through.

Taking Action After Rejection

One of the best ways to move past rejection is to take action. Rather than dwelling on what didn't work, channel your energy into what you can do next. This could mean refining your pitch, seeking feedback from trusted colleagues, or exploring new opportunities. Taking proactive steps helps you regain momentum and keeps you from getting stuck in the negative emotions that can accompany rejection.

Rejection and setbacks don't define your success; your response to them does. Each one is an opportunity to grow, refine your approach, and build resilience. With the right mindset and actions, setbacks become part of your journey toward greater achievement.

The Calm Leader in a Storm

In business, crises are inevitable. Whether it's a sudden market shift, a major financial challenge, or internal conflict, every leader will eventually face moments of intense pressure. How you handle these situations can define your success as a leader and the resilience of your organization. The ability to remain calm under pressure is not just a valuable trait; it's an essential one. Being a calm leader in the storm reassures your team, stabilizes decision-making, and prevents chaos from spreading.

The Power of Composure

When chaos strikes, emotions can easily take over. It's natural to feel stressed or overwhelmed, but a great leader knows how to keep those feelings in check. Remaining composed, even in the face of uncertainty, projects confidence and control. Your team looks to you for guidance during tough times, and if they see panic, it will only heighten their anxiety. On the other hand, a calm demeanor instills a sense of security. It reassures everyone that there's a plan, even if the path forward isn't yet clear.

Composure doesn't mean suppressing your emotions or pretending everything is fine. It means managing your reactions, staying focused, and not letting fear dictate your actions. This mindset allows you to think clearly and make better decisions, even when the pressure is at its highest.

Clear Decision-Making in Chaos

A calm leader can sift through the noise and focus on what really matters. In times of crisis, it's easy to become distracted by the many urgent problems at hand. However, the best leaders know how to prioritize and break down complex situations into manageable pieces. By staying calm, you can assess the situation more clearly, identify the most critical issues, and tackle them one at a time.

Moreover, calm leaders are better at gathering input from others before making decisions. Panic can lead to impulsive actions, while a composed approach allows for thoughtful consideration of different perspectives. By taking the time to listen to key advisors or team members, you can ensure your decisions are based on sound reasoning rather than rushed judgment.

Setting the Tone for Your Team

As a leader, your behavior sets the tone for your entire organization. In a crisis, the team will often mirror your emotions. If you're calm and composed, they're more likely to stay focused and productive. If you're visibly stressed or panicked, that energy will spread, leading to mistakes and miscommunication.

Part of leading calmly is also maintaining open lines of communication. Keep your team informed about what's happening, what steps are being taken, and what's expected of them. Clear, consistent communication prevents rumors or assumptions from taking over, which can otherwise escalate stress.

Additionally, showing empathy goes a long way. People are more likely to follow a leader who acknowledges their concerns and stresses during difficult times. Demonstrating that you understand and care about the well-being of your team helps foster trust and unity, even when the going gets tough.

The Long-Term Benefits of Calm Leadership

Staying calm in a storm is not just about surviving a crisis; it's about setting your business up for long-term success. Teams that experience calm and steady leadership during tough times are more likely to be loyal and motivated in the future. They will trust in your ability to guide them through future challenges, which builds stronger cohesion and resilience within the organization.

Moreover, consistently handling pressure with grace enhances your reputation as a leader. Colleagues, clients, and partners will recognize your ability to maintain focus and deliver results under difficult circumstances, making you a more reliable and trusted figure in the business world.

Ultimately, calm leadership is about more than just appearing unfazed. It's about providing stability, fostering clear decision-making, and leading your team through uncertainty with confidence and clarity. The storm will pass, but the strength of a calm leader endures, setting the course for long-term success.

Cultivating a Resilient Mindset

In the fast-paced world of business, challenges and setbacks are inevitable. What separates those who thrive from those who give up is their ability to cultivate a resilient mindset. Resilience is more than just bouncing back after a failure; it's about staying adaptable, maintaining optimism, and pushing forward when the road gets tough. Building this mindset takes conscious effort, but it's an essential skill for long-term success.

Embracing Challenges as Opportunities

One of the cornerstones of a resilient mindset is the ability to see challenges not as obstacles, but as opportunities for growth. When faced with a difficult situation, rather than focusing on what's going wrong, ask yourself what you can learn from it. Each challenge offers a chance to improve your skills, develop new strategies, or find innovative solutions.

Reframing challenges in this way shifts your perspective. Instead of seeing them as failures or setbacks, you begin to approach them as essential steps in your journey. This mindset reduces the fear of failure because each obstacle becomes a learning opportunity, not a dead end.

Maintaining Optimism in Difficult Times

A resilient mindset is grounded in optimism, but not in blind positivity. It's about having a realistic view of challenges while maintaining confidence that things can and will improve. This kind of optimism helps you stay focused on long-term goals, even when immediate circumstances seem difficult.

To cultivate optimism, practice focusing on what's within your control. In tough situations, it's easy to become overwhelmed by external factors you can't change. By focusing on the areas where you have influence, you'll feel more empowered and motivated to take action. Optimism isn't about ignoring the negatives—it's about believing in your ability to handle them and move forward.

Adapting to Change

Flexibility is another key aspect of resilience. In business, things don't always go as planned, and those who can quickly adapt to new circumstances are the ones who succeed. Cultivating a resilient mindset means being open to change, adjusting your plans when necessary, and not clinging to one way of doing things.

When faced with unexpected changes, ask yourself: What new opportunities could this bring? This shift in thinking helps you remain agile and proactive, rather than resistant or reactive. The more adaptable you become, the easier it is to navigate uncertainties without losing momentum.

Building a Strong Support System

Even the most resilient individuals need a support system. Resilience doesn't mean going through challenges alone—it means knowing when to lean on others. Surround yourself with mentors, peers, or colleagues who can offer guidance, feedback, and encouragement when you need it most.

Having a strong network of supportive people not only helps you gain perspective but also provides practical solutions you may not have thought of. Your network can remind you of your strengths when you're feeling unsure, and their advice can help you tackle challenges from different angles. Knowing you're not alone in facing adversity makes it easier to stay resilient in tough times.

Cultivating Self-Awareness and Self-Care

Resilience starts from within. Developing self-awareness allows you to recognize when you're feeling stressed or overwhelmed, so you can take steps to care for your mental and emotional well-being. This might mean taking breaks when needed, practicing mindfulness, or engaging in activities that recharge you.

Self-care is often overlooked in the business world, but it's essential for maintaining resilience. You can't perform at your best if you're running on empty. By taking care of your physical and mental health, you build the foundation for sustained resilience, allowing you to face challenges with a clear and focused mind.

A resilient mindset is not something you're born with; it's something you can build over time. By embracing challenges, staying optimistic, adapting to change, leaning on your support system, and practicing self-care, you'll develop the mental toughness needed to succeed in any business environment. The journey may not always be easy, but resilience will help you keep moving forward, no matter what obstacles arise.

Chapter 4

Timing is Everything

Recognizing Market Opportunities

Recognizing market opportunities is one of the most critical skills in business. It's the ability to see potential where others might only see challenges, to spot the emerging trends before they fully take shape, and to know when the time is right to act. Whether you're launching a new product, expanding into a new region, or refining your services, being able to identify and seize the right market opportunities can be the difference between success and stagnation.

Understanding Market Needs

At the heart of every market opportunity is a need. Successful entrepreneurs and business leaders have a keen ability to identify unmet needs in the marketplace. These might be pain points that customers are currently facing, or gaps in existing products or services that you can fill. To do this, you must maintain a strong connection with your customer base. Listen carefully to their feedback, complaints, and desires. Often, opportunities come from recognizing what your target audience is asking for but not yet receiving.

Additionally, paying attention to shifts in customer behavior can reveal new needs. For example, as more people embraced digital services, businesses that offered convenient online solutions, like food delivery apps or e-commerce platforms, were able to capitalize on that shift early.

Spotting Emerging Trends

Trends are constantly shaping markets, and those who can recognize them early are often the ones who gain the most. This requires staying informed about the broader economic, social, and technological shifts that influence your industry. For instance, the rise of remote work during the pandemic opened doors for businesses in sectors like online collaboration tools, virtual meeting software, and home office furniture.

To spot trends, look beyond your immediate industry. Pay attention to how other industries are evolving, and think about how those changes might impact your own. Technological advancements in one field often create ripple effects in others. Being proactive about learning what's coming next will put you in a position to capitalize on new developments before your competitors.

Timing the Market

Even if you recognize an opportunity, timing is everything. Acting too early can leave you waiting for demand to catch up, while acting too late can mean missing the wave altogether. Successful businesses often strike a balance between these two extremes, entering the market when conditions are ripe for growth.

A well-timed market entry usually involves a deep understanding of your industry's life cycle. Some industries are constantly evolving, while others are slower to change. Understanding where your market is in its cycle can help you gauge the best time to introduce a new product or service. For example, entering a market just as it's reaching maturity may require a different approach than breaking into one that is still in its early stages of growth.

Leveraging Data and Analytics

In today's world, data is an invaluable resource for recognizing market opportunities. Companies that can gather and analyze customer data effectively are often able to predict trends and consumer needs before they become obvious. Using tools like customer surveys, website analytics, and market research reports, you can uncover patterns that point toward new opportunities.

For instance, if your data shows a growing interest in sustainability among your customers, that might indicate an opportunity to develop eco-friendly products or offer sustainable alternatives to existing offerings. The key is to turn raw data into actionable insights.

Keeping an Eye on Competitors

Your competitors can also be a rich source of market opportunity insights. By closely watching how your competitors are moving within the market, you can identify gaps in their offerings or areas where they are falling short. These gaps can often become your opportunities.

For example, if a competitor launches a product that's well-received but fails to address certain customer needs, that's your chance to offer a more complete solution. Staying aware of your competitive landscape allows you to stay one step ahead and find opportunities they might have missed.

Remaining Adaptable

Finally, one of the most important aspects of recognizing market opportunities is staying flexible. Markets can change quickly, and what looked like an opportunity today might not exist tomorrow. Successful business leaders remain adaptable, ready to pivot when necessary and seize new chances as they arise. This requires a willingness to reevaluate your strategies and remain open to unexpected opportunities that may arise from changing market conditions.

Recognizing market opportunities is about staying informed, being aware of your customers' needs, and positioning yourself at the right place at the right time. With the right combination of insight, timing, and adaptability, you can spot the opportunities that will drive your business forward.

Knowing When to Walk Away

One of the hardest decisions in business is knowing when to walk away from a deal, project, or partnership. It's natural to want to push through challenges and avoid failure, but sometimes the smartest move is to cut your losses and move on. The key to making this decision lies in recognizing the warning signs early and trusting your instincts when it becomes clear that continuing will do more harm than good.

Recognizing the Signs

The first step in knowing when to walk away is paying attention to the red flags that indicate something isn't working. These signs can take many forms: a deal that consistently drags on with no progress, a business relationship that's become toxic, or a project that repeatedly misses deadlines and drains resources. If you find yourself constantly trying to fix the same problems with little success, it may be a sign that the situation is beyond saving.

Another common indicator is when the costs begin to outweigh the benefits. Whether those costs are financial, emotional, or related to time and energy, it's important to evaluate whether the effort you're putting in is leading to any meaningful returns. If every step forward feels like a struggle and you're not seeing any positive momentum, it might be time to reconsider.

Letting Go of Sunk Costs

One of the biggest psychological barriers to walking away is the concept of sunk costs—the money, time, or effort you've already invested. It's easy to think, "I've already put so much into this, I can't quit now." However, holding on to something just because of past investments can lead to even greater losses down the road. In business, success often requires the ability to make tough decisions, even when it means letting go of something you've worked hard on.

The key is to focus on future potential rather than past investment. Ask yourself: Will continuing down this path improve the situation, or is it just delaying the inevitable? By separating your emotions from the decision and evaluating it based on logic and potential outcomes, you can make a clearer choice about whether to walk away.

Trusting Your Gut

In business, data and analysis are crucial, but intuition also plays a role. Sometimes, even when the numbers don't show it, you'll have a gut feeling that something isn't right. Trusting your instincts can be just as important as relying on hard facts. If something feels off—whether it's the behavior of a potential business partner, the direction of a project, or the terms of a deal—it's worth listening to that internal signal.

Successful entrepreneurs and business leaders often attribute their best decisions to a combination of logic and intuition. Walking away from an opportunity might feel counterintuitive at first, but if your instincts are telling you that the risks are too high or the fit isn't right, it's often best to listen.

Walking Away with Grace

Knowing when to walk away doesn't mean burning bridges. In fact, how you exit a situation is just as important as the decision to leave. Leaving with professionalism and grace can preserve relationships and open doors for future opportunities. Communicate clearly and respectfully, explaining your reasoning without placing blame or creating unnecessary conflict.

By maintaining a positive, forward-focused attitude, you leave room for potential collaborations in the future. Business is rarely a one-time transaction, and how you handle difficult decisions can shape your reputation for years to come.

Ultimately, walking away isn't about giving up—it's about recognizing when a situation no longer serves your goals and having the courage to make a better choice. It's a skill that, once developed, can save you from unnecessary frustration and lead you toward opportunities that are a better fit for your time, energy, and resources.

The Right Time to Expand

Deciding when to expand your business is one of the most important decisions you'll face as an entrepreneur or business leader. Expansion can bring growth, new opportunities, and increased revenue, but if done prematurely or without proper planning, it can strain your resources and potentially harm your business. Knowing when the time is right requires a blend of strategic thinking, market awareness, and a clear understanding of your own business's readiness.

Strong Demand for Your Product or Service

One of the clearest signs that it's time to expand is when you consistently see strong demand for your product or service that outpaces your ability to supply it. If customers are waiting in line, products are selling out, or you're turning down opportunities because you lack the capacity to meet demand, expansion might be the logical next step. This indicates that the market is signaling a need for more, and your business is well-positioned to meet that demand.

However, it's crucial to distinguish between temporary surges in demand and long-term, sustainable growth. An increase in sales during a holiday season, for example, may not justify permanent expansion. Look for consistent trends in demand over a longer period before making the decision.

Financial Stability

Before expanding, your business should be on solid financial footing. Expansion requires a significant investment of resources, whether in new locations, additional staff, or increased inventory. If your business is currently struggling to maintain cash flow or cover operational costs, it's likely too early to expand. On the other hand, if you have steady, reliable profits and a healthy balance sheet, you may be ready to take the next step.

One practical way to assess your financial readiness is to conduct a thorough financial analysis, evaluating whether your current profits can support the costs of expansion without jeopardizing your existing operations. Expansion typically involves upfront costs, and a clear financial plan will help ensure you're prepared for the initial outlay as well as any potential setbacks.

Clear Market Opportunity

A successful expansion depends on more than just internal readiness; there must also be a clear market opportunity. Research is essential here. Expanding into new markets—whether geographic, demographic, or product-based—requires an understanding of the demand in that area. Are there enough potential customers to support your growth? Is the competition manageable? Are there gaps in the market that you can fill?

Answering these questions will help you determine whether the time is right to expand.

Market research can provide insights into potential areas for growth, helping you avoid costly mistakes. Expanding into a saturated market or one where demand is uncertain can drain your resources without yielding the results you expect.

Capacity for Operational Scaling

Another key factor to consider is whether your business operations can scale smoothly. This means evaluating your systems, processes, and workforce. Are your current operations running efficiently, or are there bottlenecks and inefficiencies that could worsen with expansion? A business that operates well on a small scale can struggle when trying to replicate that success on a larger scale.

If your internal processes are solid, and you have the ability to increase production, sales, or service delivery without sacrificing quality, then you may be ready for expansion. It's also worth considering whether you have the right team in place to manage growth, both at the leadership level and in day-to-day operations.

Ability to Mitigate Risks

Expansion always comes with risks, from financial challenges to operational disruptions. It's important to identify and plan for these risks before moving forward. Do you have a contingency plan if sales don't meet expectations in the new market? Can your business survive if the expansion doesn't go as planned? Being prepared to manage the risks associated with growth is crucial for long-term success.

A measured approach to expansion, such as starting with a pilot program or smaller-scale rollout, can help mitigate some of the risks. This way, you can test new markets, processes, or products without overcommitting your resources.

Personal and Leadership Readiness

Lastly, consider whether you, as a leader, are ready for the challenges of expansion. Growth often requires a shift in how you manage the business, with greater complexity, more employees to oversee, and additional responsibilities. Expanding too soon without the leadership bandwidth to handle increased demands can lead to burnout or poor decision-making.

Take stock of your leadership team and ensure that you have the right people in place to handle growth. Delegation becomes even more important as your business grows, and surrounding yourself with a capable team will ensure that expansion doesn't overwhelm your capacity to lead effectively.

Recognizing the right time to expand involves a combination of strong market signals, financial health, operational readiness, and leadership capacity. By carefully evaluating these factors, you can ensure that your expansion is strategic and sustainable, setting the stage for long-term success.

Chapter 5

The Ethics of Profit

Balancing Integrity and Profit

In business, the pressure to prioritize profit is always present. After all, without profit, no company can survive or grow. However, the pursuit of profit shouldn't come at the expense of integrity. Balancing these two forces—profit and ethics—is a challenge many business leaders face, and getting it right can be the key to long-term success.

The Role of Integrity in Business

Integrity is about more than just following laws and regulations; it's about doing what's right even when no one is watching. It's the foundation of trust, both within your organization and with your customers. Without integrity, even the most profitable ventures can crumble under the weight of bad decisions. Reputation takes years to build but can be destroyed in moments by unethical actions.

Companies that prioritize integrity build stronger relationships with their employees, partners, and customers. Employees are more engaged when they work for a business that aligns with their values. Customers are more loyal to brands they believe are ethical, and partners are more likely to collaborate with businesses that operate transparently and honestly.

Profit Without Compromise

The idea that ethics and profit are at odds is a common misconception. In reality, maintaining integrity can drive profits over the long term. Ethical practices attract customers who value responsible business operations. For example, consumers are increasingly drawn to companies that demonstrate social responsibility, environmental stewardship, and fair treatment of workers. Businesses that commit to these values often see increased customer loyalty, higher brand reputation, and, ultimately, better financial performance.

Additionally, making decisions based on integrity helps avoid costly legal issues, fines, and reputational damage. Short-term gains from cutting corners or engaging in unethical practices may bring immediate profit, but the long-term costs can far outweigh those benefits. Legal battles, public relations disasters, and lost trust can be expensive, both financially and in terms of brand equity.

Leading with Values

Business leaders who emphasize both integrity and profit lead by example. Their decisions reflect a commitment to doing what is right, even when it's difficult. This type of leadership fosters a culture of ethical behavior within the organization. When employees see that their leaders are willing to make tough choices to uphold company values, they are more likely to follow suit.

Leading with values also means being transparent with stakeholders. When companies are open about their practices, processes, and decisions, it builds trust. Customers, investors, and employees appreciate honesty, especially when it comes to difficult situations. Being upfront about challenges and how you plan to address them demonstrates accountability, which is a key aspect of integrity.

Finding the Right Balance

Balancing integrity and profit requires constant vigilance. It's about making decisions that align with your core values, even when there are easier or more profitable paths available. This doesn't mean avoiding profit; it means seeking ways to achieve financial success while staying true to your principles.

One way to maintain this balance is by setting clear ethical guidelines for your business. Establish a code of conduct that outlines acceptable practices, and ensure that everyone in the organization understands it. Encourage open communication, so employees feel comfortable reporting concerns or unethical behavior. Regularly revisit these guidelines to adapt to new challenges and opportunities without compromising your company's integrity.

Ultimately, businesses that manage to balance integrity with profit create sustainable success. They build trust with their customers, inspire loyalty in their employees, and avoid the pitfalls that come with unethical practices. Profit and integrity are not mutually exclusive; when aligned, they create a foundation for lasting growth and success.

Corporate Social Responsibility (CSR) as a Growth Tool

CSR is no longer just a buzzword or a feel-good initiative; it's a powerful growth tool that businesses can use to expand their impact while simultaneously building their brand. Today's consumers are more conscious about the ethical practices of the companies they support, and businesses that align with these values often find themselves gaining more loyal customers, enhancing their reputation, and even opening up new markets. But CSR isn't just about doing good—it's about strategically integrating these efforts into your business model for sustainable growth.

Building Trust and Loyalty

Consumers today are more aware than ever of the social and environmental impact of their purchases. When a company demonstrates that it's committed to something beyond profits—whether it's reducing its carbon footprint, supporting fair labor practices, or giving back to the community—it builds trust with its audience. Trust is the foundation of customer loyalty, and loyal customers are more likely to stick with your brand over time, even when competitors offer lower prices or flashier products.

By integrating CSR into your business, you show your customers that their values align with your company's mission. This creates an emotional connection that strengthens their loyalty and turns them into advocates for your brand. It's not just about attracting new customers; it's about building a lasting relationship with the ones you already have.

Attracting Talent and Investors

CSR isn't just attractive to consumers—it's also appealing to talented professionals and investors. Top talent increasingly wants to work for companies that reflect their personal values, especially Millennials and Gen Z employees, who place a high priority on social responsibility. When your company is known for its commitment to making a positive impact, it becomes easier to attract and retain motivated, engaged employees who want to be part of something bigger than just making profits.

Similarly, socially responsible companies often attract more investment. Many investors today are looking for businesses that have sustainable, long-term growth potential, and CSR initiatives demonstrate that your company is forward-thinking. Investors understand that companies focused on ethical practices are more likely to adapt to future challenges and regulatory changes, making them a safer bet.

Expanding into New Markets

CSR can also open doors to new market opportunities. Consumers in emerging markets, in particular, are becoming more selective about which businesses they support. Companies that invest in improving the quality of life in these regions— whether through ethical sourcing, environmental sustainability, or community development—can establish themselves as leaders in those markets.

For instance, companies that prioritize sustainable practices might find themselves with an advantage in markets where environmental regulations are tightening. By being ahead of the curve, businesses can avoid costly changes later and position themselves as responsible market leaders.

Strengthening Brand Reputation

A strong CSR strategy helps build a positive brand image, which can lead to greater visibility and a competitive edge. In the age of social media, news about a company's CSR efforts can spread quickly, increasing brand awareness and drawing in new customers. Companies known for their ethical practices and community contributions tend to be viewed more favorably by the public, media, and even industry regulators.

A well-executed CSR program can also help mitigate damage during times of crisis. Businesses that have established a reputation for doing good can draw on that goodwill during tough times, helping to cushion the impact of negative press or challenges. When consumers believe in your company's values, they're more likely to give you the benefit of the doubt when problems arise.

Incorporating CSR into your business is not just a matter of ethics, it's a strategic growth tool. Companies that prioritize social responsibility build trust with customers, attract top talent, appeal to investors, and expand into new markets. More than ever, businesses that take CSR seriously are positioned for long-term success, creating value not only for shareholders but for society as a whole.

Avoiding the Trap of Cutting Corners

In the fast-paced world of business, the temptation to cut corners is ever-present. Whether it's to save time, reduce costs, or meet tight deadlines, shortcuts can seem like a quick solution. However, while cutting corners may offer immediate gains, it often leads to long-term consequences that can severely damage your business. Avoiding this trap requires discipline, foresight, and a commitment to doing things the right way, even when it's difficult.

The Illusion of Short-Term Gains

At first glance, cutting corners can seem harmless. Maybe it's skipping a step in quality control, using cheaper materials, or bypassing a regulatory requirement. These decisions may save time or money in the moment, but they rarely hold up over time.

What seems like a smart move today can quickly turn into a costly mistake.

When businesses cut corners, they often fail to consider the hidden costs. For instance, delivering a product without thorough quality testing might result in customer complaints, returns, or even product recalls. What initially saved time can lead to reputational damage, legal issues, and higher costs in the long run. The short-term savings rarely outweigh the long-term risks.

Compromising Quality and Trust

One of the most significant dangers of cutting corners is that it compromises quality. In business, quality is everything. Customers expect products and services to meet certain standards, and when those standards aren't met, trust erodes. Losing customer trust is one of the hardest things to recover from, and once it's gone, it's often gone for good.

Take, for example, a company that decides to switch to a cheaper supplier without fully vetting their products. The result could be inferior goods that fail to meet customer expectations. While the initial decision to cut costs might seem like a smart business move, it risks damaging your brand's reputation in a way that could take years to repair.

Maintaining high standards in all aspects of business—whether it's production, customer service, or ethics—builds trust and loyalty. Cutting corners may offer a temporary advantage, but it undermines the very foundation that sustains long-term business success.

The Ripple Effect

The impact of cutting corners extends beyond just the immediate task at hand. It sets a precedent within the organization. When leaders or managers signal that it's okay to take shortcuts, it can spread throughout the company culture. Employees may begin to adopt similar practices, believing that speed and cost-cutting are more important than quality or ethics.

Once this mentality takes hold, it becomes difficult to reverse. A culture of cutting corners leads to mistakes, decreased morale, and an overall decline in performance. Over time, it erodes the values that define a successful and sustainable business.

The Value of Doing Things Right

Avoiding the trap of cutting corners starts with a commitment to doing things the right way, even when it's harder or takes longer. This doesn't mean avoiding efficiency or seeking smarter ways to work. It's about understanding that there are no real shortcuts to success. Quality, trust, and integrity must be prioritized over quick wins.

Leaders play a crucial role in this. By setting a clear example and holding everyone accountable for maintaining high standards, you create a culture where quality and ethical behavior are non-negotiable. This type of culture not only helps you avoid the pitfalls of cutting corners, but it also attracts loyal customers, reliable partners, and dedicated employees.

In the long run, businesses that prioritize doing things right, rather than cutting corners, build stronger foundations that can withstand challenges and grow sustainably. The choice to maintain integrity over speed or profit is what separates successful businesses from those that struggle to last.

Chapter 6

The Unseen Cost of Success

Burnout Among Business Leaders

Burnout is a significant and growing issue among business leaders. The pressure to meet high expectations, make critical decisions, and manage complex operations can take a toll on both mental and physical health. While the drive to succeed often pushes leaders to work harder and longer hours, this relentless pace can lead to exhaustion, decreased productivity, and even serious health problems. Recognizing the signs of burnout and learning how to manage it is crucial for sustaining long-term success.

The Causes of Burnout

Burnout among business leaders typically stems from several factors. One of the most common is the sheer volume of responsibilities. As a leader, you're expected to handle everything from strategic decision-making to team management, often while juggling deadlines and financial pressures. Over time, this constant workload can become overwhelming.

Another key contributor to burnout is isolation. Many leaders feel that they cannot show vulnerability or share the pressures they face with others, which can lead to a sense of loneliness. Being at the top can sometimes mean that you have fewer peers to confide in, leading to increased stress and anxiety.

Additionally, the rapid pace of today's business world—fueled by constant connectivity and the expectation of being "always on"—makes it difficult for leaders to disconnect. Emails, meetings, and phone calls often extend into evenings and weekends, leaving little time for rest and recovery.

Recognizing the Symptoms

The symptoms of burnout can manifest in various ways. Emotional exhaustion is one of the most common indicators, where leaders feel drained, both mentally and emotionally, to the point where they can no longer engage with their work or team in a meaningful way. This can be accompanied by a sense of cynicism or detachment, where leaders feel disconnected from their goals or question the value of their work.

Physical symptoms also play a role. Chronic fatigue, headaches, sleep disturbances, and even more severe health issues such as heart disease can be linked to prolonged stress. Often, leaders push these symptoms aside, viewing them as the cost of doing business. However, ignoring these warning signs only worsens the problem over time.

The Impact on Business

Burnout doesn't just affect the leader personally; it can have a profound impact on the entire organization. When a leader is burned out, decision-making suffers. Stress can cloud judgment, leading to hasty or poor decisions. Burnout also reduces creativity, making it harder to come up with innovative solutions to problems. Additionally, leaders who are burned out are more likely to disengage from their teams, leading to lower morale and productivity across the organization.

Moreover, the long-term health consequences of burnout can force leaders to take time off or even step down from their positions, creating instability within the company. Retaining a healthy work-life balance is essential not only for the leader's well-being but also for the continued success of the business.

Strategies for Managing Burnout

Preventing and managing burnout requires conscious effort. One of the most effective strategies is setting clear boundaries between work and personal time. This includes taking time to unplug from work regularly, ensuring that there are periods when emails, calls, and meetings are not allowed to intrude. Prioritizing rest and recovery—whether through sleep, hobbies, or spending time with loved ones—helps replenish energy and clear the mind.

Leaders should also delegate effectively. Trying to do everything on your own is a fast track to burnout. By trusting team members and empowering them to take on more responsibility, leaders can reduce their workload while also fostering growth within the team.

Building a support network is equally important. Whether through mentors, peers, or even professional counselors, having someone to talk to about the pressures of leadership can provide valuable perspective and emotional support. Sharing challenges and seeking advice helps to alleviate some of the isolation that often accompanies leadership roles.

Finally, adopting mindfulness and stress-reduction practices, such as meditation or regular physical exercise, can help mitigate the effects of stress. These practices allow leaders to stay grounded, manage their emotions more effectively, and maintain a clear mind, even in the face of challenging situations.

Burnout is a serious issue, but with the right strategies, it can be managed and even prevented. By recognizing the signs early and taking proactive steps, business leaders can protect both their health and their business's future.

Sacrifices That Shouldn't Be Made

In the pursuit of success, business leaders often face difficult choices. Long hours, personal sacrifices, and intense focus are sometimes necessary to achieve major goals. However, not every sacrifice is worth making. Certain aspects of life and well-being should never be compromised, no matter how ambitious your business objectives may be. Knowing what's truly non-negotiable can protect your health, relationships, and long-term success.

Sacrificing Health

It's easy to fall into the trap of neglecting your health when building a business. Skipping meals, sacrificing sleep, and pushing through illness may seem like ways to get more done in the short term, but they come at a heavy cost. Poor health choices can lead to burnout, chronic stress, and long-term physical problems, which can ultimately hinder your ability to perform at your best.

When leaders prioritize their health, they're not just taking care of themselves; they're ensuring their ability to lead effectively. Healthy habits—regular exercise, balanced nutrition, and sufficient rest—are not luxuries but essentials for maintaining energy, focus, and resilience. Sacrificing your health for business might yield short-term gains, but it can have long-term consequences that are much harder to reverse.

Sacrificing Relationships

Another area where business leaders often make sacrifices is in their personal relationships. Long work hours and constant focus on growing a company can leave little time for family, friends, or significant others. Over time, this neglect can strain even the strongest relationships.

While success in business requires dedication, it's important to remember that personal connections are a critical part of a fulfilling life. Healthy relationships provide emotional support, balance, and a sense of purpose beyond work. Sacrificing relationships for business may lead to regret later, especially if success comes at the cost of loneliness or fractured connections with loved ones. Maintaining strong relationships not only enriches your personal life but also contributes to your overall well-being, making you a more effective leader.

Sacrificing Personal Values

Compromising your personal values in the name of success is another sacrifice that should never be made. In business, there are often temptations to cut corners, bend ethical guidelines, or engage in practices that don't align with your principles. While these decisions might offer immediate benefits, they can lead to regret and damage your reputation over time.

Staying true to your values, even when it's difficult, builds long-term trust and respect. Businesses that operate with integrity tend to attract loyal customers, dedicated employees, and partners who share similar values. Compromising your principles for short-term gains may harm your business in the long run, especially when trust is lost. Success achieved at the expense of integrity is rarely sustainable or fulfilling.

Sacrificing Mental Well-Being

Mental well-being is often overlooked when striving for business success. The pressure to meet deadlines, exceed goals, and push through challenges can lead to overwhelming stress.

Sacrificing mental health for the sake of progress is not only damaging to your personal life but also to your work performance.

Leaders who neglect their mental health risk burnout, anxiety, and even depression, which can have a ripple effect on their decision-making and leadership abilities. Prioritizing mental well-being by managing stress, taking breaks, and seeking support when needed ensures you stay grounded and capable of handling challenges. Mental health isn't just a personal matter—it's essential for leading effectively.

Sacrifices are an inevitable part of building a business, but some things should never be put on the line. Health, relationships, personal values, and mental well-being are the foundations of a successful life, and protecting them ensures that the success you build is both meaningful and sustainable.

Sustainable Success

In business, the term "success" is often associated with growth, profit, and recognition. However, the pursuit of these goals without considering sustainability can lead to burnout, instability, or even failure in the long run. Sustainable success, on the other hand, is about building a business that not only thrives in the short term but remains resilient and prosperous over time. It's about creating a balanced approach that nurtures both the business and the people behind it.

Building a Strong Foundation

Sustainable success starts with a strong foundation. This means developing solid business practices that can withstand market fluctuations, competition, and unexpected challenges. Rather than chasing rapid, unsustainable growth, a business focused on sustainable success invests in careful planning, consistent execution, and long-term strategies. This includes building financial reserves, fostering a strong company culture, and ensuring that operational processes are efficient and scalable.

Additionally, businesses that prioritize sustainability often have a clear mission and vision that guide their decision-making. Knowing your "why" helps to stay focused on the core values that drive your business, even as external circumstances change. This clarity allows for decisions that not only seek profit but also ensure the well-being of the company and its stakeholders.

Prioritizing People

At the heart of any successful business are the people—employees, customers, partners, and even the broader community. Sustainable success relies on maintaining strong relationships with all of these groups. This involves treating employees well, creating a positive work environment, and fostering growth opportunities within the company. When employees feel valued and supported, they are more engaged and committed, which directly contributes to the company's longevity.

The same principle applies to customers. Sustainable businesses focus on building loyal customer bases by offering high-quality products and services and maintaining strong communication channels. By putting customer satisfaction at the center of your business strategy, you create lasting relationships that are more resilient to market changes or competition.

Embracing Adaptability

One of the key elements of sustainable success is adaptability. The business world is constantly evolving, with new technologies, shifting consumer preferences, and changing market conditions. A business that remains rigid in its practices risks falling behind. Sustainable success requires an openness to change and a willingness to innovate.

This doesn't mean chasing every new trend, but rather staying informed and being prepared to pivot when necessary. Whether it's adopting new technologies, entering new markets, or adjusting your business model, adaptability ensures that your business remains relevant and competitive over time.

Balancing Growth and Stability

Sustainable success involves finding the right balance between growth and stability. Rapid growth can be exciting, but if it's not supported by the right infrastructure and resources, it can lead to overextension. Many businesses grow too quickly without ensuring that their operations, finances, and team are ready to handle the expansion.

A sustainable approach focuses on steady, manageable growth that doesn't compromise the business's core stability. This means expanding at a pace that allows you to maintain quality, retain key talent, and manage resources effectively. It's about thinking long-term, rather than making short-term decisions that could jeopardize future success.

Long-Term Vision

Ultimately, sustainable success is about having a long-term vision for your business. While short-term gains are important, they should not come at the expense of the company's future. Businesses that focus on sustainability invest in the future, whether through developing their workforce, enhancing their product offerings, or contributing to the community. This approach not only leads to more resilient businesses but also helps create a legacy that can last well beyond immediate financial goals.

In essence, sustainable success is about playing the long game. It requires a combination of solid foundations, people-focused practices, adaptability, and a clear vision for the future. By embracing these principles, businesses can not only achieve success but ensure it lasts for years to come.

Chapter 7

The Power of Small Wins

Celebrating Milestones

In the world of business, the journey toward big goals is often a long and challenging one. As you work tirelessly to achieve those grand visions, it's easy to overlook the small wins along the way. However, celebrating milestones, no matter how small, is crucial for maintaining momentum, boosting morale, and fostering a sense of accomplishment among your team. These celebrations not only recognize progress but also provide the fuel needed to keep pushing forward.

Why Celebrating Matters

Milestones mark significant steps toward your ultimate goal. Whether it's reaching a sales target, launching a new product, or signing a major client, these moments deserve recognition. Celebrating them creates a sense of achievement, allowing you and your team to pause and reflect on the hard work that got you there. It's a way of acknowledging progress, which is particularly important when the end goal still feels distant.

Celebrations also have a positive psychological impact. They reinforce good habits and behaviors, encouraging people to stay committed. When a team feels their efforts are valued and appreciated, it strengthens their motivation and drive. Celebrating wins—no matter how big or small—reminds everyone that progress is happening, and that the work they're doing is making a difference.

Building Team Morale

For teams, celebrating milestones is about more than just recognition; it's about building camaraderie and boosting morale. Business can be tough, and the road to success often comes with setbacks and challenges. Pausing to celebrate a milestone gives the team a chance to come together, reflect on the journey, and appreciate each other's contributions.

These moments of celebration can strengthen team bonds, helping to create a positive work environment where people feel connected to each other and the business's mission. It reinforces a culture where achievements are shared and celebrated as a collective effort. Whether it's a simple acknowledgment in a meeting, a team lunch, or a bigger celebration, the act of coming together to mark progress energizes everyone to keep pushing toward the next goal.

Recognizing Personal Contributions

Beyond team success, milestones also provide an opportunity to recognize individual contributions. Every milestone achieved is the result of many small actions taken by different people. Celebrating these moments gives leaders the chance to highlight individual efforts, showing appreciation for the work that made the milestone possible. Personal recognition builds confidence and reinforces the importance of each person's role in the bigger picture.

When employees feel seen and valued for their efforts, it increases their sense of ownership and commitment to the company's goals. Celebrating milestones in this way not only boosts individual morale but also encourages continued dedication and hard work.

Creating a Sense of Progress

In any long-term project, the finish line can seem far away, and without recognizing smaller victories along the way, it can be easy to feel overwhelmed or discouraged. Celebrating milestones helps create a sense of progress, breaking down larger goals into achievable steps. Each celebration acts as a checkpoint, reminding the team that they are moving in the right direction and that the ultimate goal is within reach.

This sense of progress is critical for maintaining focus and energy over the long term. It helps prevent burnout and gives everyone a renewed sense of purpose after each win. By celebrating milestones, you maintain a forward momentum that keeps your team engaged and motivated.

Milestones are the markers of progress, and taking the time to celebrate them is essential for long-term success. They remind us that every step, no matter how small, brings us closer to our goals. When businesses create a culture that recognizes and celebrates these achievements, they build stronger, more motivated teams ready to take on whatever challenges lie ahead.

Building Momentum from Minor Successes

In business, big wins often make headlines, but it's the small, consistent successes that truly fuel long-term growth. Building momentum from these minor victories is one of the most powerful ways to drive your business forward. Each small achievement creates a ripple effect, giving you the energy, confidence, and resources to tackle bigger challenges. The key is recognizing these small wins and using them to propel your next move.

Celebrating Small Wins

One of the most important steps in building momentum is taking the time to recognize and celebrate minor successes. Whether it's landing a new client, hitting a modest sales target, or completing a project on time, every win counts. Acknowledging these achievements, no matter how small they may seem, helps boost morale and motivates you and your team to keep pushing forward.

When you celebrate small wins, you create a culture of positivity and progress. Each success reinforces the belief that the team is moving in the right direction, encouraging everyone to stay focused on the next goal. These celebrations don't need to be elaborate—sometimes a simple acknowledgment or a quick thank-you goes a long way in maintaining momentum.

Using Small Wins to Build Confidence

Minor successes can also boost confidence, both for individual leaders and their teams. In the early stages of any project or business, progress can feel slow, and the distance to your larger goals may seem daunting. However, small wins serve as proof that your efforts are paying off. They demonstrate that progress is being made, even if it's incremental.

This sense of accomplishment fuels your confidence and helps you approach larger challenges with a positive mindset. When you see that your strategies are working on a small scale, you're more likely to trust that they will also work when scaled up. Confidence is contagious, and as your team begins to see the impact of their efforts, they too will feel more capable and motivated to achieve even bigger goals.

Turning Small Victories into Bigger Opportunities

Each small success can open the door to larger opportunities. For example, a successful small-scale project with one client might lead to repeat business or a referral to other potential clients. Completing a minor milestone can unlock the next phase of a larger project or give you the financial stability to invest in new resources or initiatives.

The key is to leverage each win strategically. Rather than resting on your laurels, use the momentum from each success to propel your business toward the next objective. This may involve reinvesting profits, expanding into new markets, or scaling up operations in areas where you've already seen success. When small wins are used as stepping stones, they can lead to much larger breakthroughs.

Creating a Cycle of Continuous Progress

Building momentum from small successes creates a cycle of progress. Each minor achievement gives you the motivation and resources to take on the next challenge. Over time, these small wins add up, creating a snowball effect that drives sustained growth. The more wins you accumulate, the more confident, capable, and resilient your business becomes.

It's important to maintain this momentum by setting achievable goals and celebrating each success along the way. When small wins are treated as important milestones, they create a sense of forward motion that keeps your team engaged and focused on the bigger picture.

In the long run, it's the accumulation of these small victories that often leads to the most significant achievements. By recognizing their value and leveraging them strategically, you can build lasting momentum that drives your business toward sustainable success.

The Compound Effect in Business

The compound effect is a simple yet powerful principle: small, consistent actions, when repeated over time, create exponential growth. In business, this concept applies to nearly every area, from building relationships to improving processes. While it might be tempting to chase after quick wins, the real magic of success often lies in steady, incremental progress that builds upon itself over time.

Small Actions, Big Results

One of the core ideas behind the compound effect is that big achievements rarely happen overnight. Instead, they are the result of small, daily efforts that accumulate. For example, consistently improving customer service, even in small ways, can lead to increased customer loyalty, better word-of-mouth, and eventually higher sales. It's not the single large effort that transforms a business, but the combination of small improvements that leads to substantial growth.

Consider how compounding works in financial investments. A small investment, when allowed to grow over time, can become a large sum thanks to interest that builds on itself. In business, the same principle applies: a little progress each day can lead to massive results down the road.

The Importance of Consistency

In business, consistency is often more important than dramatic changes or breakthroughs. Whether it's showing up for your team, delivering reliable products, or sticking to your long-term vision, consistency builds trust and solidifies your reputation. Consistently excellent service makes customers return, and consistently improving your processes ensures that your business remains competitive.

It's easy to get caught up in wanting immediate results, but the compound effect teaches us that patience and persistence are key. A business that focuses on making small, consistent improvements—whether in product quality, customer experience, or operational efficiency—will see those efforts multiply over time, even if the initial gains seem small.

Applying the Compound Effect to Business Strategy

The compound effect can be applied strategically to any area of business. For instance, regularly investing in employee development may seem like a slow process at first, but over time, it leads to a more skilled and motivated workforce, which translates into higher productivity and innovation. Similarly, investing in customer relationships by providing personalized service or follow-up care may not yield immediate results, but over time, it builds a loyal customer base that drives growth through repeat business and referrals.

Another key area where the compound effect plays a role is in business networking. Building strong connections doesn't happen overnight. Regularly attending events, reaching out to peers, and nurturing relationships over time creates a wide and supportive network that can open doors to new opportunities in the future.

Avoiding the Trap of Quick Fixes

The compound effect also serves as a reminder to avoid the allure of quick fixes and shortcuts. It's easy to get distracted by the promise of fast results, but these often lead to short-term success that fades just as quickly. Businesses that rely on shortcuts often find themselves facing long-term consequences, whether it's diminished quality, damaged customer trust, or internal inefficiencies. True growth comes from patience, persistence, and the willingness to commit to a long-term vision.

Ultimately, the compound effect teaches us that success is not about taking giant leaps, but about making small, smart choices every day and sticking to them. Whether you're improving processes, building relationships, or developing products, these daily actions add up. Over time, they create momentum that drives your business forward in ways that may not be immediately noticeable, but are undeniably powerful.

Chapter 8

Innovating in a Saturated Market

Differentiating Through Customer Experience

In today's competitive market, where products and services can often be easily replicated, customer experience has become one of the most powerful ways to differentiate your business. While many companies focus solely on the quality or price of their offerings, those that stand out are the ones that invest in delivering an exceptional experience from start to finish. A great customer experience can turn a one-time buyer into a loyal advocate, driving long-term success and setting your business apart from the competition.

Understanding the Customer Journey

The foundation of creating a standout customer experience lies in understanding the full customer journey. From the moment a potential customer first encounters your brand to the point where they make a purchase—and even beyond that—the entire experience matters. Every interaction a customer has with your business, whether it's browsing your website, interacting with customer service, or receiving the product, shapes their perception of your brand.

To differentiate through customer experience, it's crucial to map out each touchpoint and identify opportunities to add value or reduce friction. This can be as simple as offering a seamless online shopping experience or providing helpful, personalized recommendations during the decision-making process. The goal is to make every step of the journey smooth, enjoyable, and aligned with your customer's needs and expectations.

Personalization as a Key Differentiator

One of the most effective ways to enhance customer experience is through personalization. Today's consumers expect more than just generic service—they want to feel like businesses truly understand their individual preferences and needs. Personalization can be as simple as addressing customers by name in communications or offering tailored product suggestions based on past purchases.

By leveraging data and insights, businesses can create a more personalized experience that makes customers feel valued and understood. For instance, many companies now use AI and machine learning to analyze customer behavior and offer personalized content, product recommendations, or discounts that are relevant to each individual. When customers feel that a business is paying attention to their specific preferences, they are more likely to develop a lasting connection with the brand.

Creating Memorable Moments

In addition to smooth, personalized service, creating memorable moments is a powerful way to differentiate your brand through customer experience. These are the small but meaningful gestures that leave a lasting impression on customers. Whether it's a hand-written thank-you note with a purchase, a surprise discount, or simply going above and beyond to solve a customer's problem, these moments of unexpected delight can turn customers into loyal brand ambassadors.

These efforts don't need to be extravagant. Often, it's the thoughtful, human touches that resonate the most. A customer who has had a memorable experience is far more likely to share their positive story with others, helping to build your brand's reputation through word of mouth.

Offering Exceptional Customer Support

No matter how good your products or services are, problems will occasionally arise. When they do, how your company responds can make or break the customer's experience. Offering exceptional customer support is one of the most critical elements of a strong customer experience. Prompt, friendly, and effective resolution of customer issues shows that your business genuinely cares about its customers and is willing to go the extra mile to ensure their satisfaction.

Whether through live chat, email, or phone support, making it easy for customers to get help when they need it is crucial. Moreover, empowering your customer service team to solve issues on the spot without complicated processes or delays ensures that customers walk away feeling heard and valued. This not only helps resolve immediate concerns but also strengthens the relationship for the future.

Consistency Across Channels

A consistent experience across all customer touchpoints is another key to differentiation. Whether a customer is interacting with your brand on social media, in a physical store, or through your website, the experience should feel cohesive. Consistency builds trust, and when customers know they can expect the same high level of service and care, no matter how they engage with your business, they are more likely to stay loyal.

In a world where customers have more choices than ever before, differentiating through customer experience is one of the most effective ways to stand out. By focusing on personalization, creating memorable moments, offering exceptional support, and ensuring consistency across all interactions, you can build a brand that customers not only choose but stay with for the long haul.

The Unspoken Rule of Simplicity

In business, the most effective solutions are often the simplest. Yet, simplicity is frequently overlooked in favor of complexity. Whether it's designing products, crafting business strategies, or managing operations, simplicity can lead to better results, faster execution, and greater customer satisfaction. The unspoken rule of simplicity is about cutting through the noise, removing unnecessary steps, and focusing on what truly matters. It's about making things easier—not just for yourself, but for your customers and team as well.

Simplicity in Products and Services

One of the clearest places where simplicity shows its value is in product design. Think of the most successful products on the market: they tend to do one thing really well. The iPhone, for example, revolutionized mobile technology by simplifying its interface, making it intuitive for users while hiding the complex systems behind the scenes. Customers don't want to be overwhelmed with options or features; they want solutions that are easy to understand and use.

Businesses that embrace simplicity in their offerings are often rewarded with loyal customers who appreciate the straightforward experience. By focusing on the essential features that solve core problems, companies can create products that are not only functional but also enjoyable to use. Stripping away unnecessary complexity makes products more accessible and, ultimately, more successful.

Simplicity in Strategy

In business strategy, simplicity is equally powerful. Many organizations fall into the trap of overcomplicating their plans, creating convoluted goals and processes that are difficult to follow. The best strategies, however, are clear and concise. They focus on a few key objectives and outline straightforward steps to achieve them.

When leaders simplify their strategies, it becomes easier for teams to execute. Clarity removes confusion, helping everyone stay aligned with the company's goals. Simplicity in strategy also allows for quicker adjustments when circumstances change, as the path forward is easier to navigate.

Operational Simplicity

Simplicity also shines in operations. Over time, businesses tend to accumulate processes, many of which become outdated or redundant. These layers of complexity can slow down decision-making and reduce efficiency. By regularly reviewing and streamlining operations, businesses can eliminate unnecessary tasks and free up resources to focus on more important activities.

For example, automating routine tasks, reducing unnecessary meetings, and simplifying communication channels can have a profound impact on overall productivity. A simpler approach to operations not only speeds things up but also makes it easier to adapt and grow as the business evolves.

The Customer Experience

Perhaps the most significant benefit of simplicity is the positive impact it has on the customer experience. Whether it's a smooth website interface, clear communication, or an easy checkout process, customers value businesses that make things simple. The easier it is for a customer to engage with your brand, the more likely they are to return and recommend it to others.

In a world where consumers are constantly bombarded with information and choices, simplicity stands out. Businesses that focus on creating a seamless, straightforward experience can cut through the clutter and win customer loyalty.

Simplicity, while often unspoken, is a fundamental rule in business that drives success. By embracing it in your products, strategy, and operations, you create an environment where clarity reigns, and complexity doesn't stand in the way of progress. The result is a more focused, efficient, and customer-friendly business.

Continuous Innovation as a Mindset

Innovation is often thought of as a one-time breakthrough or a revolutionary product, but in reality, it's a continuous process. Successful businesses don't innovate once and stop—they build innovation into their culture, making it an ongoing part of their operations. Developing a mindset of continuous innovation means always looking for ways to improve, adapt, and evolve, regardless of how successful your business may already be.

Embracing Change

At the core of continuous innovation is a willingness to embrace change. Markets shift, technology advances, and customer preferences evolve. Businesses that succeed over the long term are those that remain adaptable and open to new ideas. This mindset requires looking at change not as a threat, but as an opportunity to grow and improve. Companies that encourage this kind of thinking empower their employees to seek out better ways of doing things and remain competitive in a rapidly evolving landscape.

Leaders who promote continuous innovation encourage experimentation, knowing that not every idea will be a home run. However, the willingness to test, learn, and adapt is what allows innovation to flourish. Mistakes are seen as learning opportunities, not failures, and this attitude fosters a culture where creativity and new ideas are welcomed.

Small Innovations with Big Impact

Continuous innovation doesn't always mean creating the next groundbreaking product or technology. Often, it's the small, incremental improvements that drive lasting success. Businesses that commit to finding better ways to serve customers, streamline operations, or enhance their products can make significant strides through consistent, smaller innovations.

For example, a company might find a more efficient way to handle logistics or implement a new software tool that improves customer service. These incremental changes, when consistently applied, compound over time, leading to greater efficiency, cost savings, and improved customer satisfaction. Businesses that cultivate continuous innovation recognize that small, steady improvements can be just as valuable as larger, more dramatic changes.

Fostering a Culture of Curiosity

A mindset of continuous innovation thrives in a culture where curiosity is encouraged. Employees at all levels should feel empowered to ask questions, challenge assumptions, and explore new ideas. Creating a work environment that fosters curiosity leads to a more engaged and innovative team, where everyone feels that their ideas matter.

This culture starts at the top. Leaders who model curiosity and show a genuine interest in exploring new possibilities inspire their teams to do the same. Encouraging open dialogue, providing opportunities for learning, and rewarding creative thinking are all ways to build a culture where continuous innovation is the norm.

Staying Ahead of the Curve

Businesses that embrace continuous innovation are better equipped to stay ahead of their competition. Rather than waiting for disruption, they actively seek out new trends, technologies, and practices that can give them an edge. This proactive approach allows companies to lead the way in their industries, rather than playing catch-up.

To foster this mindset, businesses should dedicate time and resources to exploring future trends and technologies. Whether through research and development, partnerships, or simply staying informed about industry advancements, companies that invest in future-proofing themselves are better prepared for whatever changes may come.

Continuous innovation is about maintaining a forward-thinking mindset, staying adaptable, and always striving for improvement. It's not about chasing every trend or taking unnecessary risks, but about consistently looking for ways to evolve. This mindset ensures that your business remains relevant and competitive, even in a rapidly changing world.

Chapter 9

Mastering the Art of Quiet Influence

Leading Without Titles

Leadership isn't defined by a job title or formal authority. Some of the most impactful leaders aren't necessarily those with "manager" or "executive" in their job descriptions. Instead, they lead by example, influence, and their ability to inspire others. Leading without a title is about taking initiative, earning respect, and guiding a team through actions rather than authority.

Influence Through Action

Leadership without a title starts with influence. People follow those they trust, respect, and feel inspired by. When you consistently take initiative, make thoughtful decisions, and help others, you naturally gain influence. This type of leadership is based on what you do, not the position you hold.

In any work environment, there are countless opportunities to lead without waiting for a formal promotion. Volunteering to take on a challenging project, mentoring a colleague, or stepping up to solve a problem all demonstrate leadership. By taking ownership and contributing to the team's success, you set a standard others want to follow.

Building Trust and Relationships

Leaders without titles understand that trust is the foundation of any successful team. Building trust comes from being reliable, transparent, and supportive. When you consistently deliver on your promises and help others achieve their goals, people come to rely on you. Trust doesn't come from a title; it's earned through actions and integrity.

Strong leaders also invest in relationships. By developing genuine connections with coworkers, understanding their strengths, and supporting their growth, you foster a collaborative environment where people feel valued. This makes you a natural leader within the team, regardless of your formal role.

Empowering Others

Leadership without a title also involves empowering others to succeed. Instead of focusing on control, it's about lifting others up and helping them grow. Great leaders share their knowledge, provide opportunities for others to shine, and celebrate the team's successes.

Empowering others builds a culture of shared leadership, where everyone feels responsible for the team's success. When people are given the chance to contribute, they feel more engaged, motivated, and committed to achieving the team's goals. By creating this environment, you lead through influence and collaboration, not hierarchy.

Demonstrating Emotional Intelligence

Leaders without titles often excel in emotional intelligence. They're aware of their own emotions and can manage them in a way that helps, rather than hinders, their interactions with others. They're also skilled at reading the emotions of those around them, allowing them to build stronger connections, resolve conflicts, and guide the team through challenges.

Emotional intelligence is a key factor in leadership because it helps you understand what motivates people and how to navigate complex situations with empathy. A leader who can connect with others on an emotional level inspires loyalty and trust, creating a more cohesive and effective team.

Continuously Learning and Adapting

Finally, leading without a title means being committed to personal growth. The best leaders are always learning, whether through formal education, seeking feedback, or simply observing what works and what doesn't. They're adaptable, open to new ideas, and willing to improve themselves to better serve the team.

In a rapidly changing world, this mindset is critical. Leaders who are curious and willing to adapt are better equipped to handle new challenges and guide their teams through uncertainty. By showing a commitment to growth and improvement, you inspire others to do the same.

Leadership isn't about the title you hold; it's about the impact you have on those around you. When you lead through action, trust, and a focus on empowering others, you don't need a formal position to make a difference. Instead, you create an environment where leadership is shared, and success is a collective achievement.

Creating Change from Behind the Scenes

Creating change from behind the scenes may not always involve a spotlight, but its impact can be just as powerful, if not more.

In business, effective leaders often drive meaningful transformation without drawing attention to themselves. These leaders influence decisions, shape strategies, and guide the direction of the company through quiet, consistent efforts that leave a lasting imprint. While public leadership roles are often the most visible, the behind-the-scenes approach can yield profound and sustainable results.

Influencing Through Relationships

One of the most effective ways to create change behind the scenes is by building strong relationships. People are more likely to adopt new ideas or strategies if they trust the person proposing them. Developing meaningful connections with key stakeholders, decision-makers, and colleagues gives you the influence to make things happen without being in the spotlight.

Behind-the-scenes change-makers understand the value of relationships in driving progress. They invest time in listening, understanding other people's perspectives, and offering help where needed. This relationship-building not only gives them access to important conversations but also allows them to present their ideas in ways that resonate with others. When trust is established, change becomes much easier to implement.

Quietly Shaping Strategy

Behind-the-scenes leaders often play an essential role in shaping a company's strategy without publicly taking credit. They guide conversations, present ideas, and provide data or insights that steer decision-makers toward beneficial choices. Rather than pushing their agendas directly, they introduce concepts that allow others to feel ownership of the decision-making process.

This subtle approach can be highly effective because it reduces resistance. By allowing others to take the lead or think an idea was theirs, the change is implemented with less friction. The true driver of the strategy might remain behind the scenes, but their influence is crucial to the success of the initiative.

Supporting the Implementation of Change

Another key aspect of creating change behind the scenes is providing the support needed to make the change stick. This might involve mentoring others, offering behind-the-scenes advice, or ensuring that the right resources are available. Quiet leaders often take on the role of enablers, making sure that others have the tools, confidence, and support to carry out new initiatives.

In this way, they are like the foundation of a building—unseen but essential to keeping everything standing. By working quietly to ensure the success of others, they create lasting changes within the organization.

Driving Cultural Shifts

Cultural change is one of the hardest transformations to achieve in any business, and it often happens slowly and quietly. Behind-the-scenes leaders are well-positioned to drive cultural shifts by modeling the behaviors and values they want to see. They may not give grand speeches or make bold declarations, but through their daily actions, they influence others.

For example, if a leader wants to foster a more collaborative work environment, they might start by encouraging teamwork in their own department or subtly shifting how meetings are conducted. Over time, these small actions create a ripple effect that transforms the broader company culture without the need for a formal mandate.

Creating change from behind the scenes requires patience, subtlety, and a deep understanding of human behavior. It's about guiding others, shaping strategies, and supporting initiatives in a way that ensures lasting impact—without the need for recognition or a title. These quiet leaders may not always be in the spotlight, but their influence runs deep, and their contributions often shape the direction of the entire organization.

The Subtle Art of Persuasion

Persuasion is not about force or manipulation. It's about guiding people toward a decision that aligns with their interests while also meeting your goals. The most effective forms of persuasion are often subtle, working through empathy, trust, and emotional intelligence rather than overt pressure. Mastering this subtle art can elevate your influence in any business setting, allowing you to lead conversations, negotiate deals, and inspire action without creating resistance or tension.

Understanding the Other Person's Perspective

The foundation of subtle persuasion lies in understanding the other person's point of view. Before you can influence someone, you need to know what motivates them, what they care about, and what challenges they're facing. By stepping into their shoes, you gain insight into how to frame your argument in a way that resonates with them.

This approach requires active listening. Rather than jumping into a conversation with your own agenda, take the time to listen carefully to what the other person is saying. What are their concerns? What are their goals? When you truly understand their perspective, you can tailor your message to show how your idea or proposal aligns with their needs.

Building Trust and Credibility

People are far more likely to be persuaded by someone they trust. Trust isn't built overnight, but small, consistent actions can establish credibility over time. Being reliable, honest, and transparent in your interactions sets the stage for effective persuasion. When others know they can count on you to follow through and tell the truth, they become more open to your ideas.

Credibility also comes from demonstrating expertise. If you're knowledgeable about the topic at hand and can provide clear, well-reasoned insights, people will naturally defer to your opinion. However, it's important to avoid arrogance or overwhelming the other person with too much information. Subtle persuasion works best when you share your expertise in a way that is helpful and non-threatening.

Finding Common Ground

Another key aspect of subtle persuasion is finding common ground. When people feel that you understand them and share their values or goals, they're more likely to be open to your perspective. This doesn't mean compromising your own position, but rather identifying areas of agreement that create a foundation for collaboration.

For example, if you're negotiating a business deal, focus first on shared goals—such as mutual growth or improving customer satisfaction—before discussing any points of disagreement. By starting from a place of alignment, you set a cooperative tone that makes the other person more receptive to your ideas.

Using Emotional Appeal

While logic and facts are important, emotions play a powerful role in decision-making. Subtle persuasion often involves appealing to the emotions that drive people's choices, whether that's a desire for success, fear of missing out, or a need for connection. By tapping into these emotions, you can make your argument more compelling.

For instance, if you're trying to convince a colleague to adopt a new approach, you might highlight the potential benefits not just in terms of efficiency, but also how it could reduce stress or increase their sense of accomplishment. Emotional appeals work because they speak to people's deeper motivations, helping them see the value in your perspective on a personal level.

Offering Solutions, Not Demands

A crucial element of subtle persuasion is offering solutions rather than making demands. When you present your ideas as helpful suggestions or opportunities, rather than ultimatums, people are more likely to feel empowered and open to change. This approach fosters collaboration and reduces defensiveness.

For example, instead of saying, "We need to change this," you might frame your suggestion as, "What if we tried this new approach? It could make things easier." By positioning your idea as a way to solve a problem or improve a situation, you make it more appealing and less confrontational.

Mastering the subtle art of persuasion requires empathy, patience, and a deep understanding of human behavior. By building trust, finding common ground, and appealing to emotions, you can guide others toward decisions that benefit both sides without relying on pressure or force. In doing so, you become a more effective leader, influencer, and collaborator.

Chapter 10

Success Without Sacrificing Values

The True Definition of Success

Success is often viewed through a narrow lens—measured by titles, wealth, or status. However, the true definition of success goes far beyond these external markers. It is deeply personal, shaped by your values, goals, and what brings you fulfillment. Defining success for yourself means breaking away from societal expectations and focusing on what genuinely matters to you.

Success as Fulfillment, Not Achievement

Many people equate success with a list of achievements: promotions, financial milestones, or accolades. While these accomplishments can be satisfying, they do not necessarily lead to a sense of fulfillment. True success is more about living a life aligned with your purpose, where your daily actions reflect your personal values. For some, this might mean building a business that makes a positive impact; for others, it could be about creating work-life balance to spend more time with family.

When you view success as something tied to fulfillment rather than external accomplishments, you start to focus on what really brings you joy and satisfaction. It shifts from achieving what society views as important to what resonates with your own sense of purpose.

Balancing Professional and Personal Life

A major aspect of true success is balance. Success in one area of life, such as work, can feel empty if it comes at the cost of your health, relationships, or personal happiness. Balancing professional ambitions with personal well-being is key to long-term satisfaction.

Many leaders and entrepreneurs experience burnout because they chase traditional markers of success without considering their personal needs. True success involves creating a life where you are not only thriving professionally but also feeling content in your personal life. This balance leads to sustained energy, creativity, and happiness.

Impact Over Recognition

Another element of true success is the impact you have on others. Instead of chasing recognition or fame, a more meaningful approach is to focus on how your work improves the lives of those around you. Whether you're leading a company, mentoring others, or contributing to your community, making a difference can be a more profound measure of success than personal accolades.

When success is viewed through the lens of service and contribution, it becomes less about competition and more about creating positive change. This shift in perspective not only brings deeper fulfillment but also leads to more sustainable, long-lasting success.

Redefining Success Over Time

The definition of success evolves throughout life. What may seem like the ultimate goal in your twenties might shift as you gain more experience and clarity about your priorities. Success isn't static; it's fluid and adaptable to where you are in life. Understanding that success is not a fixed destination allows you to embrace changes and new directions as you grow.

Ultimately, the true definition of success is personal. It's about aligning your life with your values, creating balance, and making a meaningful impact on others. Defining success on your own terms ensures that it remains authentic and fulfilling, rather than simply chasing society's expectations.

Building a Legacy, Not Just a Business

In the fast-paced world of business, it's easy to get caught up in short-term goals—quarterly profits, market share, and growth metrics. While these are important, building something that lasts requires a different mindset. True success comes not from merely running a profitable business, but from creating a legacy that extends beyond your lifetime. A legacy is built by focusing on the long-term impact your business has on people, communities, and even future generations. It's about contributing something meaningful to the world that endures long after the last transaction is made.

Focusing on Purpose Beyond Profit

At the heart of building a legacy is the realization that business is about more than just making money. It's about serving a greater purpose. Companies that prioritize their mission and values often find that profitability follows. When you focus on creating positive change—whether by solving a real-world problem, advancing social causes, or improving people's lives—you build a reputation that resonates far beyond financial statements.

Businesses with a clear purpose tend to inspire loyalty, not just from customers, but from employees as well. People are more likely to support and invest in a company that stands for something they believe in. By creating a sense of purpose that goes beyond profit, you lay the foundation for a legacy that others will carry forward.

Investing in People and Culture

Building a legacy means investing in people—both within your organization and in the broader community. Businesses that last understand that their employees are their most valuable asset. By fostering a positive, growth-oriented culture, you not only improve productivity but also create an environment where people feel valued and motivated to contribute to something bigger than themselves.

When employees feel connected to a company's mission, they become ambassadors for its values, helping to preserve and carry on the legacy you've built. This kind of culture extends beyond the walls of the business itself, influencing how customers, partners, and the community perceive your brand. It's through people that a company's legacy is truly sustained.

Creating Lasting Impact

Legacy-building businesses are those that leave a lasting positive impact. This could be through innovative products that change industries, philanthropic efforts that support causes, or environmentally sustainable practices that protect the planet. When your business becomes a force for good, its influence extends far beyond your immediate reach.

Leaders who focus on legacy think about how their decisions today will affect the world tomorrow. They ask themselves questions like, "How will this contribute to the long-term success of the people and communities we serve?" and "What kind of future are we helping to create?" These reflections guide their actions, ensuring that the business contributes to something greater than its own success.

Building a Business That Outlasts You

The ultimate goal of building a legacy is creating a business that continues to thrive and make a difference long after you're no longer at the helm. This requires succession planning, developing future leaders, and ensuring that your company's values and mission are embedded in its DNA. Great leaders don't just build businesses—they build teams, systems, and cultures that can operate and grow independently.

To ensure your business endures, focus on empowering others to lead with the same vision and values you've established. By creating a strong foundation that others can build upon, you ensure that the legacy lives on, even as the company evolves over time.

Legacy is about more than profit; it's about lasting impact. By focusing on purpose, people, and the long-term good your business can do, you create something that endures. That's the difference between just running a business and building a legacy.

The Legacy of Leadership

True leadership extends far beyond the individual actions and decisions made during a leader's tenure. The most impactful leaders leave behind a legacy—a lasting influence on the people, culture, and direction of the organization. A legacy of leadership isn't about personal accolades or the power you held; it's about how you shaped the future, empowered others, and created positive change that continues long after you've moved on.

Empowering Future Leaders

One of the most important aspects of a leadership legacy is the development of future leaders. Great leaders understand that their success is not measured by their own achievements, but by how they prepare others to take the reins. Empowering others, offering mentorship, and creating opportunities for growth all contribute to building a legacy that endures.

Leaders who invest in their team create a ripple effect. When you mentor and guide others, you equip them with the tools to lead and inspire the next generation. This cycle of leadership development ensures that the values and vision you instilled continue to thrive, creating a sustainable impact.

Creating a Lasting Culture

The culture you foster as a leader is another crucial element of your legacy. Culture is not just about policies or mission statements; it's the everyday behaviors, values, and attitudes that permeate the organization. Leaders who prioritize a positive, inclusive, and purpose-driven culture leave behind an environment where people feel motivated and valued, even after they are gone.

Whether it's encouraging collaboration, fostering innovation, or maintaining a strong commitment to ethical practices, a leader's influence on culture has a long-lasting effect. A strong culture creates a sense of continuity, giving teams the foundation to adapt and succeed, regardless of leadership changes.

Making Meaningful Change

Legacy is also about the lasting changes you've made. Successful leaders don't just maintain the status quo; they create meaningful, long-term improvements. Whether it's through strategic initiatives, innovations, or transforming business models, the impact of those changes should be felt for years to come.

Meaningful change is often rooted in a leader's vision. Leaders with a clear, forward-thinking perspective can guide their organizations toward new opportunities and growth. The changes you implement should not only address immediate challenges but also lay the groundwork for future success.

Impact Beyond the Organization

A true leadership legacy often extends beyond the walls of the organization. Whether through contributions to the community, industry advancements, or social impact initiatives, leaders can influence the world around them.

Leaders who use their platform to promote positive change in society leave behind a legacy that resonates on a larger scale.

This might include advocating for sustainability, supporting charitable causes, or pushing for greater diversity and inclusion. The actions you take in these areas not only benefit your organization but also reflect the broader impact of your leadership philosophy.

The legacy of leadership is about leaving something greater than yourself. It's about developing others, shaping a strong culture, and making lasting contributions that outlive your time in a leadership role. The mark of a great leader is not found in the immediate success they achieve but in the enduring influence they leave behind.

Conclusion

Throughout this book, we've explored the unspoken rules of business—those subtle but powerful principles that can shape your path to success. From understanding the art of building trust before a deal to mastering leadership without a title, these insights go beyond the conventional advice found in most business guides. We've seen how reading between the lines in contracts, leveraging customer experience, and leading with emotional intelligence can set you apart in today's competitive market.

The core message of this book is that true business success isn't just about mastering the obvious. It's about seeing the invisible forces that drive relationships, decision-making, and growth. By applying the unspoken rules, you unlock the potential to lead with confidence, build lasting partnerships, and create a sustainable, purpose-driven business.

The significance of these lessons goes beyond short-term wins. They are about building something meaningful—something that lasts. In the fast-paced world of business, where trends come and go, these principles serve as your foundation, guiding you toward long-term success, stability, and impact.

As you move forward, remember that success is not just defined by profit or growth metrics. It's defined by the legacy you build, the people you empower, and the lasting impact you leave behind. The unspoken rules of business are there for you to embrace, adapt, and apply in your own journey.

Now, it's your turn. Take the insights you've gained here and put them into action. Whether you're navigating the complexities of leadership, shaping your company's culture, or finding the right time to expand, these principles will help guide you. The path to success isn't always obvious, but with the right mindset, perseverance, and a deep understanding of these unspoken rules, you have the tools to create something extraordinary.

Your business, your success, your legacy—it's all within reach.

Dear Reader,

I hope you found the book insightful and valuable.

Your feedback is invaluable to me. If you enjoyed reading this book, I would appreciate it if you could take a moment to leave a review on the reading apps and platforms.

Thank you for your support, and I wish you all the best.

Kind regards,
Ghazwan

About the Author

Ghazwan is a passionate entrepreneur and business strategist dedicated to helping individuals and organizations achieve their full potential with a deep understanding of modern businesses' challenges and opportunities.

With a Master's degree in Computer and Systems Sciences from Stockholm University, specializing in eService design, requirement engineering, and business process management, he is equipped to innovate cutting-edge solutions.

He believes in the power of collaboration and lifelong learning, and his mission is to empower people to reach their goals and positively impact the world.

www.ingramcontent.com/pod-product-compliance
Lightning Source LLC
Chambersburg PA
CBHW071033240526
45469CB00006BD/2193